Emmanuel: The Glory of Christmas

By Max Lucado and Charles Swindoll

Copyright © 2007 by Max Lucado and Charles Swindoll

Published by Thomas Nelson, Inc., Nashville, TN 37214

All Scripture quotation in this book are from the New King James Version (NKJV) © 1979,
1980, 1982, 1992, 2002, Thomas Nelson. Inc.,
Publisher and are used by permission.

ISBN-10:1-4041-0516-6
ISBN-13: 978-1-4041-0516-4

Printed in the United States of America

The gift is not

from man to God.

It is from God to man.

Max Lucado

DAY 1

I will both lie down in peace, and sleep; for you alone,
O LORD, make me dwell in safety.
PSALM 4:8

*L*ike tiny frightened sparrows, shivering in the
winter cold, many live their lives on the barren
branches of heartbreak, disappointment, and loneli-
ness, lost in thoughts of shame, self-pity, guilt, or failure.
One blustery day follows another, and the only company
they keep is with fellow-strugglers who land on the same
branches, confused and unprotected.

We try so hard to attract them into the warmth. Week
after week church bells ring. Choirs sing. Preachers
preach. Lighted churches send out their beacon. But nothing seems to bring in those who need warmth the most.

Then, as the year draws to a close, Christmas offers its
wonderful message. Emmanuel. God with us. He who re-
sided in Heaven, co-equal and co-eternal with the Father
and the Spirit, willingly descended into our world. He
breathed our air, felt our pain, knew our sorrows, and
died for our sins. He didn't come to frighten us, but to
show us the way to warmth and safety.

CHARLES SWINDOLL
THE FINISHING TOUCH

DAY 2

And the Word became flesh and dwelt among us,
and we beheld His glory, the glory as of the only
begotten of the Father, full of grace and truth.
JOHN 1:14

There is no way our little minds can comprehend the love of God. But that didn't keep him from coming.

From the cradle in Bethlehem to the cross in Jerusalem we've pondered the love of our Father. What can you say to that kind of emotion? Upon learning that God would rather die than live without you, how do you react? How can you begin to explain such passion?

MAX LUCADO
In the Grip of Grace

DAY 3

But to each one of us grace was given
according to the measure of Christ's gift.
EPHESIANS 4:7

*I*magine coming to a friend's house who has invited you over to enjoy a meal. You finish the delicious meal and then listen to some fine music and visit for awhile. Finally, you stand up and get your coat as you prepare to leave. But before you leave you reach into your pocket and say, "Now, how much do I owe you?" What an insult! You don't do that with someone who has graciously given you a meal. Isn't it strange, though, how this world is running over with people who think there's something they must do to pay God back? Somehow they are hoping God will smile on them if they work real hard and earn his acceptance; but that's an acceptance on the basis of works. That's not the way it is with grace.

CHARLES SWINDOLL
The Grace Awakening

DAY 4

For by grace you have been saved through faith,
and that not of yourselves; it is the gift of God.
EPHESIANS 2:8

Salvation is God-given, God-driven, God-empowered, and God-originated. The gift is not from man to God. It is from God to man.

Grace is created by God and given to man . . . On the basis of this point alone, Christianity is set apart from any other religion in the world . . . Every other approach to God is a bartering system; if I do this, God will do that. I'm either saved by works (what I do), emotions (what I experience), or knowledge (what I know).

By contrast, Christianity has no whiff of negotiation at all. Man is not the negotiator; indeed, man has no grounds from which to negotiate.

MAX LUCADO
IN THE GRIP OF GRACE

DAY 5

*Then the shepherds returned, glorifying
and praising God for all the things that they
had heard and seen, as it was told them.*
LUKE 2:20

The black sky exploded with brightness. Trees that had been shadows jumped into clarity. Sheep that had been silent became a chorus of curiosity. One minute the shepherd was dead asleep, the next he was rubbing his eyes and staring into the face of an alien.

The night was ordinary no more.

The angel came in the night because that is when lights are best seen and that is when they are most needed. God comes into the common for the same reason.

His most powerful tools are the simplest.

MAX LUCADO
The Applause of Heaven

DAY 6

And let the peace of God rule in your hearts, to which
also you were called in one body; and be thankful.
COLOSSIANS 3:15

There is a practical reason Thanksgiving always precedes Christmas: It sets in motion the ideal mental attitude to carry us through the weeks in between. In other words, a sustained spirit of gratitude makes the weeks before Christmas a celebration rather than a marathon.

Maybe these few thoughts will stimulate you to give God your own thanks in greater abundance.

Thank you Lord: for your sovereign control over our circumstances, for your Word that gives us direction, for your love that holds us close, for your understanding when we are confused, and for your Spirit that enlightens our eyes.

CHARLES SWINDOLL
The Finishing Touch

DAY 7

Know the God of your father, and serve Him with a loyal
heart and with a willing mind; for the LORD searches all
hearts and understands all the intent of the thoughts.
1 CHRONICLES 28:9

From a distance, we dazzle: up close, we're tarnished. Put enough of us together and we may resemble an impressive mountain range. But when you get down into the shadowy crevices . . . the Alps we ain't.

That's why our Lord means so much to us. He is intimately acquainted with all our ways. Darkness and light are alike to him. Not one of us is hidden from his sight.

All things are open and laid bare before him: our darkest secret, our deepest shame, our stormy past, our worst thought, our hidden motive, our vilest imagination . . . even our vain attempts to cover the ugly with snow-white beauty.

He comes up so close. He sees it all. He knows our frame. He remembers we are dust. Best of all, he loves us still.

CHARLES SWINDOLL
THE FINISHING TOUCH

DAY 8

Hear me when I call, O God of my righteousness! You have relieved me in my distress; have mercy on me, and hear my prayer.
PSALM 4:1

Discipline is easy for me to swallow. Logical to assimilate. Manageable and appropriate. But God's grace? Anything but.

Examples? How much time do you have?

David the psalmist becomes David the voyeur, but by God's grace becomes David the psalmist again.

Peter denied Christ before he preached Christ.

Zacchaeus, the crook. The cleanest part of his life was the money he'd laundered. But Jesus still had time for him . . .

Story after story. Prayer after prayer. Surprise after surprise.

Seems that God is looking more for ways to get us home than for ways to keep us out. I challenge you to find one soul who came to God seeking grace and did not find it.

MAX LUCADO
WHEN GOD WHISPERS YOUR NAME

DAY 9

*Be of good courage, and He shall strengthen
your heart, all you who hope in the LORD.*
PSALM 31:24

Take from us our wealth and we are hindered. Take our health and we are handicapped. Take our purpose and we are slowed, temporarily confused. But take away our hope, and we are plunged into deepest darkness . . . stopped dead in our tracks, paralyzed. Wondering, "Why?" Asking, "How much longer? Will this darkness ever end? Does he know where I am?"

Then the Father says, "That's far enough," and how sweet it is! Like blossoms in the snow, long-awaited color returns to our life. The stream, once frozen, starts to thaw. Hope revives and washes over us.

Inevitably, spring follows winter. Every year. Yes, including this one. Barren days, like naked lambs, will soon be clothed with fresh life. Do you need that reminder today?

CHARLES SWINDOLL
The Finishing Touch

Christmas strips away

the veneer of stacked-up years

and brings us back

to where we started.

Charles Swindoll

DAY 10

Depart from evil and do good; seek peace and pursue it.
PSALM 34:14

*W*ant to see a miracle? Plant a word of love heartdeep in a person's life. Nurture it with a smile and a prayer, and watch what happens.

An employee gets a compliment. A wife receives a bouquet of flowers. A cake is baked and carried next door. A widow is hugged. A gas-station attendant is honored. A preacher is praised.

Sowing seeds of peace is like sowing beans. You don't know why it works; you just know it does. Seeds are planted, and topsoils of hurt are shoved away.

Don't forget the principle. Never underestimate the power of a seed.

MAX LUCADO
The Applause of Heaven

DAY 11

In this the love of God was manifested toward us,
that God has sent His only begotten Son
into the world, that we might live through Him.
1 JOHN 4:9

Untethered by time, [God] sees us all. From the backwoods of Virginia to the business district of London; from the Vikings to the astronauts, from the cave-dwellers to the kings, from the hut-builders to the finger-pointers to the rock-stackers, he sees us.

And he loves what he sees. Flooded by emotion. Overcome by pride, the Starmaker turns to us, one by one, and says, "You are my child. I love you dearly. I'm aware that someday you'll turn from me and walk away. But I want you to know, I've already provided a way back."

And to prove it, he did something extraordinary. What God says, God does.

CHARLES SWINDOLL
The Finishing Touch

DAY 12

Then the angel said to them, "Do not be afraid, for behold,
I bring you good tidings of great joy which will be to all people.
For there is born to you . . . a Savior, who is Christ the Lord.
LUKE 2:10–11

We worry. We worry about the IRS and the SAT and the FBI. We worry we won't have enough money, and when we have money we worry that we won't manage it well. We worry that the world will end before the parking meter expires. We worry what the dog thinks if he sees us step out of the shower. We worry that someday we'll learn that fat-free yogurt was fattening.

Honestly, now. Did God save you so you would fret? Would he teach you to walk just to watch you fall? Would he be nailed to the cross for your sins and then disregard your prayers? I don't think so either.

MAX LUCADO
In the Grip of Grace

DAY 13

But you, Bethlehem, in the land of Judah, are not the least
among the rulers of Judah; for out of you shall come a ruler
Who will shepherd My people Israel.
MATTHEW 2:6

A small cathedral outside Bethlehem marks
the supposed birthplace of Jesus. Behind a
high altar in the church is a cave, a little cavern lit
by silver lamps.

You can enter the main edifice and admire the
ancient church. You can also enter the quiet cave
where a star embedded in the floor recognizes the
birth of the King. There is one stipulation, however.
You have to stoop. The door is so low you can't go in
standing up.

The same is true of the Christ. You can see the
world standing tall, but to witness the Savior, you
have to get down on your knees.

MAX LUCADO
The Applause of Heaven

DAY 14

Your word is a lamp to my feet and a light to my path.
PSALM 119:105

A piano sits in a room, gathering dust. It is full of the music of the masters, but in order for such strains to flow from it, fingers must strike the keys . . . trained fingers, representing endless hours of disciplined dedication. You do not have to practice. The piano neither requires it nor demands it. If, however, you want to draw beautiful music from the piano, that discipline is required . . .

Light won't automatically shine upon you nor will truth silently seep into your head by means of rocking-chair osmosis.

It's up to you. It's your move.

CHARLES SWINDOLL
The Finishing Touch

When you give yourself,

the gift never has

to be returned.

Charles Swindoll

DAY 15

Be an example . . . in word, in conduct,
in love, in spirit, in faith, in purity.
1 TIMOTHY 4:12

You want to make a difference in your world?
Live a holy life:

Be faithful to your spouse.
Be the one at the office who refuses to cheat.
Be the neighbor who acts neighborly.
Be the employee who does the work and doesn't complain.
Pay your bills.
Do your part and enjoy life.
Don't speak one message and live another.

People are watching the way we act more than they are listening to what we say.

MAX LUCADO
A GENTLE THUNDER

DAY 16

So it was, when the angels had gone away from them into heaven, that the shepherds said to one another, "Let us now go to Bethlehem and see this thing that has come to pass, which the Lord has made known to us."

LUKE 2:15

*I*t was a beautiful night—a night worth peeking out your bedroom window to admire—but not really an unusual one. No reason to expect a surprise. Nothing to keep a person awake. An ordinary night with an ordinary sky.

The sheep were ordinary. Common animals. No fleece made of gold. No blue-ribbon winners. They were simply sheep—lumpy, sleeping silhouettes on a hillside.

And the shepherds. Peasants they were. Probably wearing all the clothes they owned. Smelling like sheep and looking just as woolly. They were conscientious, willing to spend the night with their flocks. But you won't find their staffs in a museum nor their writings in a library. They were nameless and simple.

And were it not for a God who loves to hook an "extra" on the front of the ordinary, the night would have gone unnoticed.

But God dances amidst the common. And that night he did a waltz.

MAX LUCADO
In the Grip of Grace

DAY 17

And Mary said: "My soul magnifies the Lord, and my spirit has rejoiced in God my Savior. For He has regarded the lowly state of His maidservant;. . .for He who is mighty has done great things for me."

LUKE 1:46–49

*T*he light of the universe entered a dark, wet womb. He whom angels worship nestled himself in the placenta of a peasant, was birthed into the cold night, and then slept on cow's hay.

Mary didn't know whether to give him milk or give him praise, but she gave him both since he was, as near as she could figure, hungry and holy.

Joseph didn't know whether to call him Junior or Father. But in the end called him Jesus, since that's what the angel had said and since he didn't have the faintest idea what to name a God he could cradle in his arms.

Don't you think . . . their heads tilted and their minds wondered, "What in the world are you doing, God?" Or, better phrased, "God, what are you doing in the world?"

MAX LUCADO
IN THE GRIP OF GRACE

DAY 18

Then Mary said to the angel, "How can this be, since I do not know a man?" And the angel answered and said to her, "The Holy Spirit will come upon you, and the power of the Highest will overshadow you; therefore, also, that Holy One who is to be born will be called the Son of God. For with God nothing will be impossible."

LUKE 1:34–35, 37

When it came time for God to send his Son to earth, he did not send him to the palace of some mighty king. He was conceived in the womb of an unwed mother—a virgin!—who lived in the lowly village of Nazareth.

In choosing those who would represent Christ and establish his church, God picked some of the most unusual individuals imaginable: unschooled fishermen, a tax collector(!), a mystic, a doubter, and a former Pharisee who had persecuted Christians. He continued to pick some very unusual persons down through the ages. In fact, he seems to delight in such surprising choices to this very day.

So let God be God. Expect the unexpected.

CHARLES SWINDOLL,
THE FINISHING TOUCH

DAY 19

But while he thought about these things, behold, an angel of the Lord appeared to him in a dream, saying, "Joseph, son of David, do not be afraid to take to you Mary your wife, for that which is conceived in her is of the Holy Spirit."

MATTHEW 1:20

Seren-dip-ity—the dip of the serene into the common responsibilities of life. Serendipity occurs when something beautiful breaks into the monotonous and the mundane. A serendipitous life is marked by "surprisability" and spontaneity.

Though I have walked with God for several decades, I must confess I still find much about him incomprehensible and mysterious. But this much I know: He delights in surprising us. He dots our pilgrimage from earth to heaven with amazing serendipities.

Your situation may be as hot and barren as a desert or as forlorn and meaningless as a wasteland. You may be tempted to think, "There's no way!" when someone suggests things could change.

All I ask is that you . . .be on the lookout. God may very well be planning a serendipity in your life.

CHARLES SWINDOLL
The Finishing Touch

DAY 20

"I have come that they may have life, and that they may have it more abundantly. I am the good shepherd. The good shepherd gives His life for the sheep."
JOHN 10:10–11

*B*ecause it is short, life is packed with challenging possibilities. Because it is uncertain, it's filled with challenging adjustments. I'm convinced that's much of what Jesus meant when he promised us an abundant life.

With each new dawn, life delivers a package to your front door, rings your doorbell, and runs. Each package is cleverly wrapped in paper with big print. One package reads: "Watch out. Better worry about this!" Another: "Danger. This will bring fear!" And another: "Impossible. You'll never handle this one!"

When you hear that ring tomorrow morning, try something new. Have Jesus Christ answer the door for you.

CHARLES SWINDOLL
THE FINISHING TOUCH

He placed his hand on the

shoulder of humanity and said,

"You're something special."

Max Lucado

DAY 21

"As the Father knows me, even so I know the Father;
and I lay down My life for the sheep. No one takes
it from Me, but I lay it down of Myself."
JOHN 10:15, 18

Can anything make me stop loving you?" God asks.
"Watch me speak your language, sleep on your
earth, and feel your hurts. Behold the maker of sight
and sound as he sneezes, coughs, and blows his nose.
You wonder if I understand how you feel? Look into the
dancing eyes of the kid in Nazareth; that's God walking
to school. Ponder the toddler at Mary's table; that's God
spilling his milk.

"You wonder how long my love will last? Find your
answer on a splintered cross, on a craggy hill. That's me
you see up there."

MAX LUCADO
In the Grip of Grace

DAY 22

Let the word of Christ dwell in you richly in all wisdom, teaching and admonishing one another in psalms and hymns and spiritual songs, singing with grace in your hearts to the Lord.
COLOSSIANS 3:16

There is something grand about old things that are still in good shape. Old furniture, rich with the patina of age and history, is far more intriguing than the uncomfortable, modern stuff. When you sit on it or eat off it or sleep in it, your mind pictures those in previous centuries who did the same in a world of candlelight, oil lamps, buggies, outhouses, and potbelly stoves. Each scrape or dent holds a story you wish you knew . . .

The Bible is old also—ancient, in fact. It's timeless stories have for centuries shouted, "You can make it! Don't quit . . . don't give up!" Its truths, secure and solid as stone, say, "I'm still here, waiting to be claimed and applied."

Though ancient, it has never lost its relevance. Though battered, no one has ever improved on its content. Though old, it never fails to offer something pure, something wise, something new.

CHARLES SWINDOLL,
THE FINISHING TOUCH

DAY 23

For I am persuaded that neither death nor life, nor angels nor
principalities nor powers, nor things present nor things to come,
nor height nor depth, nor any other created thing, shall be able to
separate us from the love of God which is in Christ Jesus our Lord.
ROMANS 8:38–39

Here is what we want to know. We want to know how long God's love will endure . . . Does God really love us forever? We want to know . . . how does God feel about me when I'm a jerk?

I want to know how he feels about me when I snap at anything that moves, when my thoughts are gutter-level, when my tongue is sharp enough to slice a rock. How does he feel about me then?

Can anything separate us from the love Christ has for us?

God answered our question before we asked it. So we'd see his answer, he lit the sky with a star. So we'd hear it, he filled the night with a choir; and so we'd believe it, he did what no man had ever dreamed. He became flesh and dwelt among us.

MAX LUCADO
In the Grip of Grace

DAY 24

And she brought forth her firstborn Son, and wrapped Him in swaddling clothes, and laid Him in a manger, because there was no room for them in the inn.
LUKE 2:7

Oh, the irony of God's delight—born in the parched soil of destitution rather than the fertile ground of achievement.

It's a different path, a path we're not accustomed to taking. We don't often declare our impotence. Admission of failure is not usually admission into joy. Complete confession is not commonly followed by total pardon. But then again, God has never been governed by what is common.

MAX LUCADO
The Applause of Heaven

DAY 25

*Search me, O God, and know my heart; try me, and
know my anxieties; and see if there is any wicked way
in me, and lead me in the way everlasting.*

PSALM 139:23–24

*I*n our world of superficial talk and casual relationships, it is easy to forget that a smile doesn't necessarily mean "I'm happy" and the courteous answer "I'm fine" may not be at all truthful . . .

I'm not suggesting that everyone is an emotional time bomb or that masks are worn by all who seem to be enjoying life. But I've lived long enough to know that many a heart hides agony while the face reflects ecstasy.

There is Someone, however, who fully knows what lurks in our hearts. And knowing, he never laughs mockingly and fades away. He never shrugs and walks away. Instead, he understands completely and stays near.

Who, indeed, knows? Our God, alone, knows. He sympathizes with our weaknesses and forgives all our transgressions. To him there are no secret struggles or silent cries.

CHARLES SWINDOLL
The Finishing Touch

DAY 26

*Eye has not seen, nor ear heard, nor have entered
into the heart of man the things which God
has prepared for those who love Him.*
I CORINTHIANS 2:9

Try this. Imagine a perfect world. Whatever that means to you, imagine it. Does it mean peace? Then envision absolute tranquility. Does a perfect world imply joy? Then create your highest happiness. Will a perfect world have love? If so, ponder a place where love has no bounds. Whatever heaven means to you, imagine it. Get it firmly fixed in your mind. Delight in it. Dream about it. Long for it.

When it comes to describing heaven, we are all happy failures.

MAX LUCADO
WHEN GOD WHISPERS YOUR NAME

When his joy invades our lives, it

spills over into everything we do and

onto everyone we touch.

Charles Swindoll

DAY 27

For we brought nothing into this world,
and it is certain we can carry nothing out.
And having food and clothing,
with these we shall be content.
1 TIMOTHY 6:7–8

Contentment is something we must learn. It isn't a trait we're born with. But the question is how?

You see, society's plan of attack is to create dissatisfaction, to convince us that we must be in a constant pursuit for something "out there" that is sure to bring happiness. When you reduce that lie to its lowest level, it is saying that contentment is impossible without striving for more.

God's Word offers the exact opposite advice: Contentment is possible when we stop striving for more. Contentment never comes from externals. Never!

CHARLES SWINDOLL
THE FINISHING TOUCH

DAY 28

*Give heed to the voice of my cry, my King
and my God, for to You I will pray.*
PSALM 5:2

*D*o you want to know how to deepen your
prayer life? Pray. Don't prepare to pray. Just
pray. Don't read about prayer. Just pray. Don't attend
a lecture on prayer or engage in discussion about
prayer. Just pray.

Posture, tone, and place are personal matters.
Select the form that works for you. But don't think
about it too much. Don't be so concerned about
wrapping the gift that you never give it. Better to pray
awkwardly than not at all.

And if you feel you should only pray when
inspired, that's okay. Just see to it that you are
inspired every day.

MAX LUCADO
WHEN GOD WHISPERS YOUR NAME

DAY 29

I wait for the LORD, my soul waits,
And in His word I do hope.
PSALM 130:5

The Scriptures are replete with references to the value of waiting for the Lord and spending time with him.

When we do, the debris we have gathered during the hurried, busy hours of our day gets filtered out, not unlike the silt that settles where a river widens. With the debris out of the way, we are able to see things more clearly and feel God's nudging more sensitively.

God still longs to speak to waiting hearts . . . hearts that are quiet before him.

CHARLES SWINDOLL
The Finishing Touch

DAY 30

Now, therefore, fear the LORD,
serve Him in sincerity and in truth.
JOSHUA 24:14

Servanthood implies diligence, faithfuness
loyalty, and humility. Servants don't
compete . . . or grandstand . . . or polish their image
. . . or grab the limelight. They know their job, they
admit their limitations, they do what they do quietly
and consistently.

Servants cannot control anyone or everything, and
they shouldn't try.

Servants cannot change or "fix" people.

Servants cannot explain many of the great things
that happen.

Servants cannot meet most folks' expectations.

Servants cannot concern themselves with who
gets the credit . . .

Let's serve . . . in the name of Jesus.

CHARLES SWINDOLL
THE FINISHING TOUCH

To order additional copies

Call 1·800·933·9673

or visit

www.nelsonministryservices.com